from
Debbie Jude
5/3/69
Farewell —

The Treasure of Friendship

THE TREASURE OF

FRIENDSHIP

Favorite Writings About

Enjoying and Keeping Friends

Selected by Peter Seymour

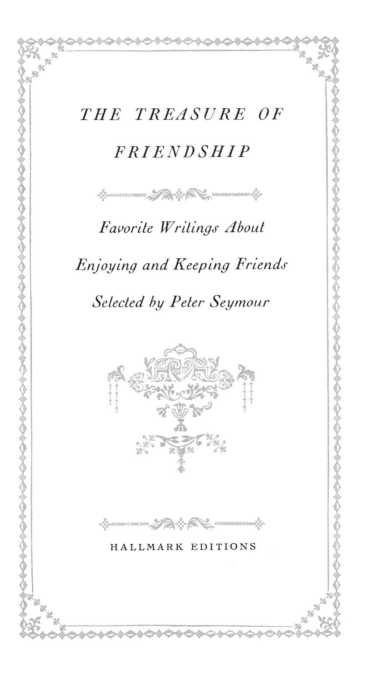

HALLMARK EDITIONS

ACKNOWLEDGMENTS

"The Art of Friendship" by Wilferd A. Peterson. Copyright 1960-1961 by Wilferd A. Peterson. "The Primary Joy" from *Peace of Mind* by Joshua Loth Liebman. Copyright 1946 by Joshua Loth Liebman. "A Friend Listens" from *A Child of the Century* by Ben Hecht. Copyright, 1954 by Ben Hecht. "On Frankness" by Robert Hillyer. Copyright 1947, 1959 by United Newspapers Magazine Corporation. "To Be A Friend" by Robert Hardy Andrews. "Friendship Mending" by Frank Morley, all reprinted by permission of Simon & Schuster, Inc., publisher. "Thank You, Friend" from *Poems of Inspiration and Courage* by Grace Noll Crowell. Copyright 1946 by Harper & Row, Publishers, Inc. "Treasured Memories" from *Wind, Sand, and Stars* by Antoine de Saint-Exupery, copyright, 1939 by Harcourt, Brace & World, Inc. Reprinted by permission of Harcourt, Brace & World, Inc. and William Heinemann Ltd. "Harry Is Alive" from *Pageant of Adventure* by Lowell Thomas and reprinted with his permission. Excerpt from p. 344 *Mark Twain's Notebook*, edited by Albert Bigelow Paine (Harper, 1935). "Truthfulness" from *The Business of Being a Friend* by Bertha Conde, copyright 1916. Reprinted by permission of Houghton Mifflin Co., publisher. "Congeniality" from *The Pleasure of Your Company* by Frances Lester Warner. Copyright, 1940 by Frances Warner Hersey. Reprinted by permission of Houghton Mifflin Co., publisher. "An Act of Faith" from *From Another World* by Louis Untermeyer. Copyright, 1939 by Harcourt, Brace & World, Inc. and reprinted with their permission. Excerpt from *The Open Door* by Helen Keller, copyright, 1957 by Helen Keller. Reprinted by permission of Doubleday & Co., Inc., publisher. "Sacrifices for Friendship" reprinted with the permission of Charles Scribner's Sons from *The New Being*, pp. 144-145, by Paul Tillich. Copyright 1955 by Paul Tillich. "Friendship's Growth" from "On Making Friends" in *Essays* by Christopher Morley. Copyright 1920, 1948 by Christopher Morley. Published by J. B. Lippincott Company. Reprinted by permission of J. B. Lippincott Company and the Estate of Christopher Morley. "The Friend Who Just Stands By" by B.Y. Williams. Copyright, 1928 by Sully and Co. Reprinted by permission of Bernice Williams Foley.

The Treasure of

Friendship

To Be A Friend

I N India 2500 years ago, a man named Gautama Buddha walked the roads and preached and taught. His teachings are still remembered by five hundred million Buddhist believers in Asia and the Orient.

I am not a Buddhist. But I find no disloyalty to my faith in accepting advice as practical today as it was when Buddha first offered it. In a mango grove in Bihar he told one of his disciples that five things are necessary to achieve release from unhappiness and fear. These, he said, include: restraint, proper discourse, energy in producing good thoughts, firmness in pursuing them, and acquisition of true insight. But first of all, and above all, he said, the seeker must learn to be a good friend.

When people asked for a definition

of friendliness, Buddha answered, »It means to have hope of the welfare of others more than for one's self . . . . It means affection unsullied by hope or thought of any reward on earth or in heaven.«

Buddha admitted that such generous wholeheartedness would not be easy. Yet in the long run it is intensely practical. »Compassion and knowledge and virtue,« he said, »are the only possessions that do not fade away.«

»To be a good friend . . .« How simple it sounds—just five short words. Yet how much they represent! Think how much it could mean, a flowing out of new forces of friendship from person to person, and eventually from land to land.

Try as we may, there is no other form of security. As Buddha said, »Friendship is the only cure for hatred, the only guarantee of peace.«

Robert Hardy Andrews

My only sketch, profile, of Heaven is a large blue sky, larger than the biggest I have seen in June—and in it are my friends—all of them—every one of them.

EMILY DICKINSON

BE slow to fall into friendship;
but when thou art in,
continue firm and constant.

SOCRATES

Beyond Words

THERE may be moments in friendship, as in love, when silence is beyond words. The faults of our friend may be clear to us, but it is well to seem to shut our eyes to them. Friendship is usually treated by the majority of mankind as a tough and everlasting thing which will survive all manner of bad treatment. But this is an exceedingly great and foolish error; it may die in a hour of a single unwise word; its conditions of existence are that it should be dealt with delicately and tenderly, being as it is a sensitive plant and not a roadside thistle. We must not expect our friend to be above humanity.

OUIDA

LIFE is a chronicle of friendship. Friends create the world anew each day. Without their loving care, courage would not suffice to keep hearts strong for life.

HELEN KELLER

Precious Friendship

F RIENDSHIP is a vase, which, when it is flawed by heat or violence or accident, may as well be broken at once; it can never be trusted after. The more graceful and ornamental it was, the more clearly do we discern the hopelessness of restoring it to its former state. Coarse stones, if they are fractured, may be cemented again; precious ones never.

WALTER SAVAGE LANDOR

Congeniality

THE pleasure of your company is a many-sided affair. It includes the pleasure of seeing you, the pleasure of hearing you talk, the drama of watching your actions, your likes and dislikes and adventures; the pleasure of hunting you up in your haunts, and the delicate flattery we feel when you hunt us up in ours. We mean all this and more when we say that we find you 'congenial'.

Congeniality, when once established between two kindred spirits or in a group, is the most carefree of human relationships. It is effortless, like purring. It is a basic theme in friendship. . . .

FRANCES LESTER WARNER

THE only way
to have a friend is to be one.

RALPH WALDO EMERSON

WHAT a thing friendship is—
World without end!

ROBERT BROWNING

The Rarest Faith

F RIENDSHIP takes place between those who have an affinity for one another, and is a perfectly natural and inevitable result. No professions or advances will avail. Even speech, at first, necessarily has nothing to do with it; but it follows after silence, as the buds in the graft do not put forth into leaves till long after the graft has taken. It is a drama in which the parties have no part to act . . . .

Friendship is never established as an understood relation. Do you demand that I be less your friend that you may know it? Yet what right have I to think that another cherishes so rare a sentiment for me? It is a miracle which requires constant proofs. It is an exercise of the finest imagination and the rarest faith. It says by a silent but eloquent behavior: »I will be so related to thee as thou canst not imagine; even so thou mayest believe. I will spend truth, all my wealth on thee,« and the friend responds silently through his nature, and life, and treats his friend with the same divine courtesy . . . .

The language of Friendship is not words but meaning. It is an intelligence above language. One imagines endless conversations with his friend, in which the tongue shall be loosed, and thoughts be spoken, without hesitancy, or end; but the experience is commonly far otherwise . . . .

Suppose you go to bid fare well to your friend who is setting out on a journey; what other outward sign do you know than to shake his hand . . . ? There are some things which a man never speaks of, which are much finer kept silent about. To the highest communications we only lend a silent ear . . . . In human intercourse the tragedy begins, not when there is misunderstanding about words, but when silence is not understood.

HENRY DAVID THOREAU

THE holy passion of Friendship is so sweet and steady and loyal and enduring a nature that it will last through a whole lifetime, if not asked to lend money.

MARK TWAIN

This Is Friendship

IT is one of the severest tests of friend-ship to tell your friend of his faults. If you are angry with a man, or hate him, it is not hard to go to him and stab him with words; but so to love a man that you cannot bear to see the stain of sin upon him, and to speak painful truth through loving words—this is friendship. But few have such friends. Our enemies usually teach us what we are, at the point of the sword.

HENRY WARD BEECHER

FRIENDSHIP is the shadow of the evening, which strengthens with the setting sun of life.

LA FONTAINE

Understanding and Trust

THE very best thing is good talk, and the thing that helps it most, is *friendship*. How it dissolves the barriers that divide us, and loosens all constraints, and diffuses itself like some fine old cordial through all the veins of life—this feeling that we understand and trust each other, and wish each other heartily well! Everything into which it really comes is good. It transforms letterwriting from a task to a pleasure. It makes music a thousand times more sweet. The people who play and sing not *at us*, but *to us*—how delightful it is to listen to them! Yes, there is a talkability that can express itself even without words. There is an exchange of thoughts and feelings which is happily alike in speech and in silence. It is quietness pervaded with friendship.

HENRY VAN DYKE

A New World

I awoke this morning with devout thanksgiving for my friends, the old and the new. Shall I not call God the Beautiful, who daily showeth himself so to me in his gifts. I chide society, I embrace solitude, and yet I am not so ungrateful as not to see the wise, the lovely and the noble-minded, as from time to time they pass my gate. Who hears me, who understands me, becomes mine— a possession for all time. Nor is Nature so poor but she gives me this joy several times, and thus we weave social threads of our own, a new web of relations; and, as many thoughts in succession substantiate themselves, we shall by and by stand in a new world of our own creation, and no longer strangers and pilgrims in a traditionary globe. My friends have to come to me unsought. The great God gave them to me.

RALPH WALDO EMERSON

Always A Friend

A true friend unbosoms freely, advises justly, assists readily, adventures boldly, takes all patiently, defends courageously, and continues a friend unchangeably. In short, choose a friend as thou dost a wife, till death separate you. Death cannot kill what never dies. Nor can spirits ever be divided that love and live in the same Divine Principle. This is the comfort of friends, that though they may be said to die, yet their friendship and society are, in the best sense, ever present, because immortal.

WILLIAM PENN

A Perfect Union

WHAT we commonly call friends and
friendships are nothing but an acquaintance and connection, contacted
either by accident or upon some de-
sign, by means of which there happens
some little intercourse betwixt our
souls. But, in the friendship I speak
of, they mingle and melt into one
piece, with so universal a mixture that
there is left no more sign of the seam
by which they were first conjoined.
If any one should ask why I loved [a
friend] I feel it could not otherwise be
expressed than by making answer,
'Because it was he; because it was I.'
There is, beyond what I am able to
say, I know not what inexplicable and
inevitable power that brought on this
union.

MONTAIGNE

Thank You, Friend

I never came to you, my
        friend,
And went away without
Some new enrichment of the heart:
More faith, and less of doubt,
More courage for the days ahead,
And often in great need
Coming to you, I went away
Comforted, indeed.

How can I find the shining words,
The glowing phrase that tells
All that your love has meant to me,
All that your friendship spells?
There is no word, no phrase for you
On whom I so depend
All I can say to you is this:
God bless you, precious friend.

GRACE NOLL CROWELL

Not in Vain

I F I can stop one heart from
breaking,
I shall not live in vain;
If I can ease one life the aching,
Or cool one pain,
Or help one fainting robin
Unto his nest again,
I shall not live in vain.

EMILY DICKINSON

FRIENDSHIP improves
happiness,
and abates misery,
by doubling our joy,
and dividing our grief.

JOSEPH ADDISON

Sacrifices for Friendship

THERE are people who believe that man's life is a continuous flight from pain and a persistent search for pleasure. I have never seen a human being of whom that is true. It is true only of beings who have lost their humanity, either through complete disintegration or through mental illness.

The ordinary human being is able to sacrifice pleasures and to take pain upon himself for a cause, for somebody or something he loves and deems worthy of pain and sacrifice. He can disregard both pain and pleasure because he is directed not towards his pleasure but towards the things he loves and with which he wants to unite.

If we desire something because of the pleasure we may get out of it, we may get the pleasure but we shall not get joy. If we try to find someone through whom we may get pleasure, we may get pleasure but we shall not have joy. If we search for something in order to avoid pain, we may avoid pain, but we shall not avoid sorrow. If we try to use someone to protect us from pain, he may protect us from pain but he will not protect us from sorrow.

Pleasures can be provided and pain can be avoided, if we use or abuse other beings. But joy cannot be attained and sorrow cannot be overcome in this way. Joy is possible only when we are driven towards things and persons because of what they are and not because of what we can get from them.

PAUL TILLICH

Accept My Full Heart's Thanks

YOUR words came just when needed.
  Like a breeze
Blowing and bringing from the
      wide soft sea
Some cooling spray, to meadow
      scorched with heat
  And choked with dust and clouds
    of sifted sand
That hateful whirlwinds, envious
      of its bloom,
    Had tossed upon it. But the
      cool sea breeze
Came laden with the odors of the sea
  And damp with spray, that laid
      the dust and sand,
And brought new life and strength
      to blade and bloom,
  So words of thine came over
      miles to me,
    Fresh from the mighty sea, a
      true friend's heart,

And brought me hope, strength,
and swept away
  The dusty webs that human
  spiders spun
Across my path. Friend—and
the word means much—
  So few there are who reach
  like thee, a hand
Up over all the barking curs of spite
  And give the clasp, when most
  its need is felt,
Friend, newly found, accept my
full heart's thanks.

ELLA WHEELER WILCOX

A Friendship Toast

MAY you live
as long as you like,
and have all that you like
as long as you live.

ANONYMOUS

The Friend Who Just Stands By

WHEN trouble comes your soul
      to try,
You love the friend who just
   »stands by.«
Perhaps there's nothing he can do—
The thing is strictly up to you;
For there are troubles all your own,
And paths the soul must tread alone;
Times when love cannot smooth the
   road
Nor friendship lift the heavy load,
But just to know you have a friend
Who will »stand by« until the end,
Whose sympathy through all endures,
Whose warm handclasp is always
   yours—
It helps, someway, to pull you through,
Although there's nothing he can do.
And so with fervent heart you cry,
»God bless the friend who just
'stands by.'«

                              B. Y. WILLIAMS

The Greatest Happiness

L IFE is to be fortified by many friendships. To love, and to be loved, is the greatest happiness. If I lived under the burning sun of the equator, it would be pleasure for me to think that there were many human beings on the other side of the world who regarded and respected me; I could not live if I were alone upon the earth, and cut off from the remembrance of my fellow-creatures. It is not that a man has occasion often to fall back upon the kindness of his friends; perhaps he may never experience the necessity of doing so; but we are governed by our imaginations, and they stand there as a solid and impregnable bulwark against all the evils of life.

SYDNEY SMITH

New Friends and Old Friends

MAKE new friends, but keep
    the old;
Those are silver, these are gold.
New-made friendships, like new wine,
Age will mellow and refine.
Friendships that have stood the test—
Time and change—are surely best;
Brow may wrinkle, hair grow gray;
Friendship never knows decay.
For 'mid old friends, tried and true,
Once more we our youth renew.
But old friends, alas! may die;
New friends must their place supply.
Cherish friendship in your breast—
New is good, but old is best;
Make new friends, but keep the old;
Those are silver, these are gold.

JOSEPH PARRY

Good Conversation

THE mind never unbends itself so agreeably as in the conversation of a well-chosen friend. There is indeed no blessing of life that is any way comparable to the enjoyment of a discreet and virtuous friend. It eases and unloads the mind, clears and improves the understanding, engenders thought and knowledge, animates virtue and good resolutions, soothes and allays the passions, and finds employment for most of the vacant hours of life.

JOSEPH ADDISON

Friendship's Growth

F RIENDSHIPS do not grow up in any carefully tended and contemplated fashion . . . . They begin haphazard.

As we look back on the first time we

saw our friends we find that generally our original impression was curiously astray. We have worked along beside them, have consorted with them drunk or sober, have grown to cherish their delicious absurdities, have outrageously imposed on each other's patience—and suddenly we awoke to realize what had happened.

We had, without knowing it, gained a new friend. In some curious way the unseen border line had been passed. We had reached the final culmination of Anglo-Saxon regard when two men rarely look each other straight in the eyes because they are ashamed to show each other how fond they are.

We had reached the fine flower and the ultimate test of comradeship—that is, when you get a letter from one of your » best friends,« you know you don't need to answer it until you get ready to.

Christopher Morley

Old Friends

O ld friends are the great blessing of one's latter years. Half
a word conveys one's meaning. They
have a memory of the same events,
and have the same mode of thinking. I
have young relations that may grow
upon me, for my nature is affectionate,
but can they grow old friends?

HORACE WALPOLE

A Friend Listens

I have noted that the best and
closest friends are those who
seldom call on each other for help. In
fact, such is almost the finest definition of a friend—a person who does
not need us but who is able to enjoy us.

I have seldom suffered over the
troubles of a friend. Are his mishaps

30

short of tragedy, I am inclined to chuckle. And he is seldom serious in telling me of his misfortunes. He makes anecdotes out of them, postures comically in their midst and tries to entertain me with them. This is one of the chief values of my friendship, as it is of his. We enable each other to play the strong man superior to his fate. Given a friend to listen, my own disasters change color. I win victories while relating them. Not only have I a friend » on my side« who will believe my version of the battle—and permit me to seem a victor in my communiques—but I have actually a victory in me. I am able to show my friend my untouched side. My secret superiority to bad events becomes stronger when I can speak and have a friend believe in it.

BEN HECHT

An Act of Faith

THE quality of friendship, unlike that of mercy, is continually being strained. But it is the essence of friendship that it can stand the strain. Friendship is like love at its best: not blind but sympathetically all-seeing; a support which does not wait for understanding; an act of faith which does not need, but always has, reason.

LOUIS UNTERMEYER

The Warmth of Friendship

A s you say, we don't need soft skies to make friendship a joy to us. What a heavenly thing it is; »World without end,« truly. I grow warm thinking of it, and should glow at the thought if all the glaciers of the Alps were heaped over me! Such friends God has given me in this little life of mine!

CELIA THAXTER

A slender acquaintance with the world must convince every man that actions, not words, are the true criterion of the attachment of friends; and that the most liberal professions of goodwill are very far from being the surest marks of it.

GEORGE WASHINGTON

'Harry Is Alive'

A t Las Vegas, New Mexico, Carl Myers spoke up and said: » The Carnegie Medal? What do I care about the medal? Harry is alive, isn't he?« Yes, Harry Reid was alive, and that was reward enough for Carl Myers.

They were both miners, and they planted eleven charges of dynamite in an eighty-five foot shaft. They cut the fuses long enough so they'd be able to climb up to a higher level, where they'd be safe from the blast. Then they lighted the fuses and ran. Carl scampered up the incline. But before Harry could make it, one charge of dynamite went off prematurely, and hurled him down, unconscious, hundreds of splinters piercing his legs. Carl yelled to him. No response. And there were those other ten charges of dynamite, fuses lighted and sputtering! If they exploded with Harry down there, that would be the end of Harry.

Carl took a jump down the incline. The fuses were burning short, the dynamite might go any minute. Carl picked up his unconscious pal, flung him across his shoulder, and started up the steep twenty-five foot slope. It was a muscle-breaking job—he had to go mighty fast. Just as he got to the top to safety, dumped Harry down and fell exhausted—the dynamite roared.

The mine owners announced that they were going to recommend Carl Myers for the Carnegie Award for Heroism. But Carl just growled:— »Damn the medal, Harry is alive, isn't he?«

LOWELL THOMAS

Friend of a Wayward Hour

F RIEND of a wayward hour,
        you came
Like some good ghost, and went
    the same;
And I within the haunted place
Sit smiling on your vanished face
    And talking with—your name.
But thrice the pressure of
your hand—
First hail—congratulations—and
Your last »God bless you!« as
    the train
That brought you snatched you
    back again
    Into the unknown land.
»God bless me?« Why, your
    very prayer
Was answered ere you asked it there,
I know—for when you came to lend
Me your kind hand, and call me friend,
    God blessed me unaware.

                JAMES WHITCOMB RILEY

To Our Guest

IF you come cheerily,
Here shall be jest for you;
If you come wearily,
Here shall be rest for you.
If you come borrowing,
Gladly we'll loan to you;
If you come sorrowing,
Love shall be shown to you.
Under our thatch, friend,
Place shall abide for you;
Touch but the latch, friend,
The door shall swing wide for you!

NANCY BYRD TURNER

37

The Art of Friendship

THE first step in the art of friendship is to be a friend; then making friends takes care of itself. To be a friend a man should start by being a friend to himself, by being true to his highest and best and by aligning himself with the enduring values of human life that make for growth and progress.

To be a friend a man should strive to be »like the shadow of a great rock in a weary land,« to be a source of refuge and strength to those who walk in darkness.

To be a friend a man should believe in the inherent goodness of men and in their potential greatness; he should treat men in a big spirit, expectant of a noble response.

To be a friend a man should strive to lift people up, not cast them down; to encourage, not discourage; to set an example that will be an inspiration to others.

To be a friend a man should be sensitively responsive to the dreams and aims of others and should show sincere appreciation for the contributions others make to the enrichment of his life.

To be a friend a man should practice the companionship of silence and the magic of words that his speech may build and not destroy, help and not hinder.

To be a friend a man should close his eyes to the faults of others and open them to his own.

To be a friend a man should not attempt to reform or reprimand, but should strive only to make others happy if he can.

To be a friend a man should be himself, he should be done with hypocrisy, artificiality and pretense, he should meet and mingle with people in quiet simplicity and humility.

To be a friend a man should be tolerant, he should have an understanding heart and a forgiving nature, knowing that all men stumble now and then, and that he who never made a mistake never accomplished anything.

To be a friend a man should join hands with all people who are working for great principles, great purposes and great causes; he should put his shoulder to the wheel to help achieve common goals.

To be a friend a man should go more than halfway with his fellow men; he should greet others first and not wait to be greeted; he should radiate a spirit of overflowing good will.

To be a friend a man should remember that we are human magnets; that like attracts like, and that what we give we get.

To be a friend a man should recognize that no man knows all the answers, and that he should add each day to his knowledge of how to live the friendly way.

WILFERD A. PETERSON

The Habit of Friendship

A s widowers proverbially mar-
ry again, so a man with the
habit of friendship always finds new
friends. . . . My old age judges more
charitably and thinks better of mankind than my youth ever did. I
discount idealization, I forgive one-
sidedness, I see that it is essential to
perfection of any kind. And in each
person I catch the fleeting suggestion
of something beautiful, and swear
eternal friendship with that.

GEORGE SANTAYANA

THE proper office of a friend is to side
with you when you are in the wrong.
Nearly anybody will side with you
when you are in the right.

MARK TWAIN

Truthfulness

EVERY friendship that lasts is built of certain durable materials. The first of these is truthfulness. If I cannot look into the eyes of my friend and speak out always the truthful thought and feeling with the simplicity of a little child, there can be no real friendship between us. Friends who have to be »handled« or »managed«, or with whom we take refuge in fencing or posing, do not know the love that casts out fear. »Trust is the first requisite for making a friend,« says Hugh Black,—»faithfulness is the first requisite for keeping him«; and trust and faithfulness cannot endure without truthfulness.

BERTHA CONDE

On Frankness

*I was angry with my friend: I told my
wrath, my wrath did end.*

WILLIAM BLAKE

I have found that these lines in a poem by Blake are well worth remembering. Often they have helped me meet the little but galling irritations which arise because of something that somebody has said or done to me.

It is so easy to misinterpret the words and deeds of others. Conversely, one must be a very tactful person indeed to avoid offending someone else in the course of a busy day. And when such slips occur, it is all too easy for the victim to nurse his pride in silence and cultivate the seeds of enmity with a thousand midnight suspicions.

How can we expect understanding between nations when individuals—

friends and kin—are so jumpy?

In my own life, I have found that the answer lies in Blake's couplet. Tell your wrath—but not wrathfully. Find out what is wrong.

Often it turns out that there is some very simple answer. Perhaps I misunderstood my friend entirely. Or perhaps I had unconsciously hoarded up several small resentments of which this one became the climax. Or possibly my friend, nervous and irritable himself, had a momentary impulse to annoy me, which by now he regrets. Whatever the cause, » talking it out« generally made the trouble disappear.

The next two lines in Blake's poem tell what happens if you follow the opposite course:

> *I was angry with my foe:*
> *I told it not, my wrath did grow.*

So unless you really wish to nurse your wrath, letting your good friend

become your bitter enemy—and that
is a very grave decision—you had better let him know, at once, exactly
what is on your mind.

Tell your wrath. Just three words.
But, believe me, they are words to live
by.

ROBERT HILLYER

Comfortably Together

M Y coat and I live comfortably
together.
It has assumed all my wrinkles, does
not hurt me anywhere, has moulded
itself on my deformities, and is com-
placent to all my movements, and I
only feel its presence because it keeps
me warm. Old coats and old friends
are the same thing.

VICTOR HUGO

The Arrow and The Song

I shot an arrow
into the air,
It fell to earth, I know not where;
For, so swiftly it flew, the sight
Could not follow it in its flight.

I breathed a song into the air,
It fell to earth, I knew not where;
For who has sight so keen and strong,
That it can follow the flight of song?

Long, long afterward, in an oak
I found the arrow, still unbroke;
And the song, from beginning to end,
I found again in the heart of a friend.

HENRY WADSWORTH LONGFELLOW

WHAT is friendship? One soul in two
bodies.

ARISTOTLE

The Primary Joy

THE primary joy of life is acceptance,
approval, the sense of appreciation
and companionship of our human
comrades. Many men do not understand that the need for fellowship is
really as deep as the need for food,
and so they go throughout life accepting many substitutes for genuine,
warm, simple relatedness.

JOSHUA LOTH LIEBMAN

An Agreeable Friend

WHEN I was eight years old and
was spending a weekend vis-
iting my Aunt Libby Linsley at her
home in Stratford on the Housatonic,
a middleaged man called one evening,
and after a polite skirmish with my
aunt, he devoted his attention to me.
At that time, I happened to be excited

about boats, and the visitor discussed the subject in a way that seemed to me particularly interesting. After he left, I spoke of him with enthusiasm. What a man! And how tremendously interested in boats! My aunt informed me he was a New York lawyer; that he cared nothing whatever about boats—took not the slightest interest in the subject. »But why then did he talk all the time about boats?«

»Because he is a gentleman. He saw you were interested in boats, and he talked about the things he knew would interest and please you. He made himself agreeable.«

I never forgot my aunt's remark.

WILLIAM LYON PHELPS

In Constant Repair

I have often thought that as
longevity is generally de-
sired, and I believe generally expected,
it would be wise to be continually add-
ing to the number of our friends, that
the loss of some may be supplied by
others.

Friendship,» the wine of life,«should
be like a well-stocked cellar, be thus
continually renewed; and it is consola-
tory to think, that although we can
seldom add what will equal the generous first-growth, yet friendship becomes insensibly old in much less time
than is commonly imagined, and not
many years are required to make it
very mellow and pleasant.

Warmth will, no doubt, make con-
siderable difference. Men of affectionate temper and bright fancy will
coalesce a great deal sooner than those
who are cold and dull. This [proposi-

tion] was the opinion of [Dr. Samuel] Johnson himself. He said to Sir Joshua Reynolds, »If a man does not make new acquaintances through life, he will soon find himself left alone. A man, Sir, should keep his friendships in constant repair.«

James Boswell

Friendship's Freedom

THE love of friendship should be gratuitous. You ought not to have or to love a friend for what he will give you. If you love him for the reason that he will supply you with money or some other temporal favor, you love the gift rather than him. A friend should be loved freely for himself, and not for anything else.

St. Augustine

Tokens of Love

G ET not your friends by bare
compliments, but by giving
them sensible tokens of your love. It
is well worthwhile to learn how to win
the heart of man the right way. Force
is of no use to make or preserve a
friend, who is an animal that is never
caught and tamed but by kindness
and pleasure. Excite them by your
civilities, and show them that you desire nothing more than their satis-
faction; oblige with all your soul that
friend who has made you a present of
his own.

SOCRATES

Friendship Mending

A man, Sir, should keep his friendships in constant repair.

SAMUEL JOHNSON

T HESE words from Johnson entered into me as a boy and ever since then have quietly exerted a power of compulsion. I think it was the oddness of the wording which first startled me. Was friendship a thing to be repaired, as if with hammer and nails? Did Johnson mean you should consciously go around, as politicians do, mending fences? I thought I knew what friendship was, and that when it occurred it was just natural, not something to be carpentered.

Yet the simple and puzzling phrase stayed in my mind till suddenly one day the meaning came clear: You can't take friendship for granted. It always needs repair. Cross your two

fingers—and even people as close as
that can lose touch. They can drift
apart. Friendship is something you
can't buy and can't command, but
you can lose. So it must be refreshed.
At all times, and before too late, it
needs refreshment.

How, then, does one go about re-
freshing friendship? »On clean-shirt
day,« wrote Johnson's biographer,
»he went abroad, and paid visits.«
That was his way. But to my mind the
specific details of repairing friendship
are not very important. Sound friendships consist of many nameless acts.
What matters is the intent—the intent to keep alive something worthy
and mutual. This happens when people remember each other, cultivate
each other, meet each other a little
more than halfway. Such are the ways
in which friendship may be shared.

Nothing on earth is more important, for, just as it has been said that
»to lose a friend is to die a little,« so

the reverse is also true, and when you keep a friend you add something to the richness and the worth of life.

FRANK V. MORLEY

Interest In People

You can make more friends in two months by becoming really interested in other people, than you can in two years by trying to get other people interested in you. Which is just another way of saying that the way to make a friend is to be one.

DALE CARNEGIE

Woman As Friend

IT is a wonderful advantage to a man,
in every pursuit or avocation, to se-
cure an adviser in a sensible woman.
In woman there is at once a subtle
delicacy of tact, and a plain soundness
of judgment, which are rarely com-
bined to an equal degree in man.

A woman, if she be really your
friend, will have a sensitive regard for
your character, honor, repute. She
will seldom counsel you to do a shabby
thing; for a woman friend always de-
sires to be proud of you. At the same
time, her constitutional timidity makes
her more cautious than your male
friend. She, therefore, seldom counsels
you to do an imprudent thing. By
friendships, I mean pure friendships,
—those in which there is no admixture
of the passion of love, except in the
married state.

A man's best female friend is a wife of good sense and good heart, whom he loves, and who loves him. If he have that, he need not seek elsewhere. But suppose the man to be without such a helpmate, female friendship he must have, or his intellect will be without a garden, and there will be many an unheeded gap even in its strongest fence.

Better and safer, of course, are such friendships, where disparities of years or circumstances put the idea of love out of the question. Middle life has rarely this advantage: youth and age have. Moliere's old housekeeper was a great help to his genius; and Montaigne's philosophy takes both a gentler and loftier character of wisdom from the date in which he finds, in Marie de Gournay, an adopted daughter.

SIR EDWARD BULWER-LYTTON

Small Service

S MALL service is true service
  while it lasts;
  Of friends, however humble, scorn
    not one;
The daisy, by the shadow that it
  casts,
  Protects the lingering dewdrop
    from the sun.

WILLIAM WORDSWORTH

Treasured Memories

OLD friends cannot be created out of
hand. Nothing can match the treasure
of common memories, of trials en-
dured together, of quarrels and recon-
ciliations and generous emotions. . . .
We forget that there is no hope of joy
except in human relations.

ANTOINE DE SAINT-EXUPERY

A Friend's Greeting

I'D like to be the sort of friend
    that you have been to me;
I'd like to be the help that you've been
    always glad to be;
I'd like to mean as much to you each
    minute of the day
As you have meant, old friend of mine,
    to me along the way.

I'd like to do the big things and the
    splendid things for you,
To brush the gray from out your skies
    and leave them only blue;
I'd like to say the kindly things that I
    so oft have heard,
And feel that I could rouse your soul
    the way that mine you've stirred.

I'd like to give you back the joy that
    you have given me,
Yet that were wishing you a need I
    hope will never be;

I'd like to make you feel as rich as I,
  who travel on
Undaunted in the darkest hours with
  you to lean upon.

I'm wishing as the days go on that I
  could but repay
A portion of the gladness that you've
  strewn along my way;
And could I have one wish this year,
  this only would it be:
I'd like to be the sort of friend that
  you have been to me.

Edgar A. Guest

Friend and Partner

It is the individual who is not interested in his fellow man who has the
greatest difficulties in life and pro-
vides the greatest injury to others. It
is from among such individuals that
all human failures spring. All that we
demand of a human being, and the

highest praise we can give him, is that
he should be a good fellow worker, a
friend to all other men, and a true
partner in love and marriage.

ALFRED ADLER

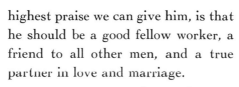

Set in Sonderdruck, a unique
Roman type from the Ludwig & Mayer
foundry. It blends harmoniously
with the 18th Century fleurons
from the Andrew Szoeke collection
used in this edition. Printed on
Hallmark Eggshell Book paper.
Designed by Harald Peter.